I0482056

Breaking Down Bitcoin

A study of Bitcoin and the Shari' Hukm Related to it

A.C. Ahmed
www.facebook.com/acahmed.page

istinarah Press

Istinarah Press

www.maktabaislamia.com
info@maktabaislamia.com
www.facebook.com/everythingislamic
www.twitter.com/maktabaislamia

2018 CE – 1439 H

Translation of the Qur'ān

It should be perfectly clear that the Quran is only authentic in its original language, Arabic. Since perfect translation of the Quran is impossible, we have used the translation of the meaning of the Quran throughout the book, as the result is only a crude meaning of the Arabic text.

Qur'ānic verses appear in speech marks proceeded by a reference to the Surah and verse number. Sayings (*Hadith*) of Prophet Muhammad ﷺ appear in inverted commas along with reference to the Hadith Book and its Reporter.

صلى الله عليه وسلم - ﷺ (Peace be upon him)
سبحانه وتعالى - ﷻ (Glory to Him, the Exalted)

Contents

Every writer will perish,
But Time will preserve what his hands did write.
So write not with your script anything except
That which on Resurrection will be a pleasing sight!

INTRODUCTORY REMARKS

This study aims to address the reality of Bitcoin and crytpocurrencies and provide some insight as regards to the Islamic legal viewpoint relating to them. I shall outline the origins and theory behind Bitcoin aswell as providing an assessment of it from an Islamic viewpoint based on my understanding as a student of Islamic Jurisprudence.

There are currently already some Islamic papers and works, all of which I encourage readers of this paper to also read. Namely, I recommend the following:

1. *"The reality of cryptocurrencies such as Bitcoin and the shari'ah rule regarding them"* by Ustadh Abu Khaled[1]

2. *"Bitcoin: Shariah Compliant?"* by Mufti Faraz Adam;[2]

3. *"The Islamic Ruling on Bitcoin"* by Shiekh Ata bin Khalil Abu al-Rashdah.[3]

Whilst they contain certain differing views as to the permissibility of Bitcoin, it should be understood that they all provide a helpful starting point for those who wish to sincerely understand the different positions reached to date. We thank them for their contribution to the area in terms of Islamic jurisprudence and for allowing us as students to develop through evaluating

---

[1] http://islamicsystem.blogspot.com.es/2017/06/the-reality-of-cryptocurrencies-such-as.html

[2] https://afinanceorg.files.wordpress.com/2017/08/research-paper-on-bitcoin-mufti-faraz-adam.pdf

[3] https://plus.google.com/100431756357007517653/posts/5MZfuRFPwwa

their legal reasoning. We make dua that Allah (swt) blesses them and their work and keeps them sincere. Differences in such issues must not lead to violating the dignity of others, no matter how mistaken their conclusions or method of reasoning may seem to us. Mufti Faraz's paper is not intended to constitute a fatwa (as the disclaimer therein states) whereas those of Ustadh Abu Khaled and Sheikh Ata are regarded to be their *ijtihad* on the matter. To the extent that they are correct in their findings we hope that Allah (swt) will reward them, and even if they are mistaken we hope that they will not be deprived of reward, although this does not rule out differing with them and pinpointing gaps in their analysis. If through analysing and study, based on the reality and the evidences from Islam, it appears that Bitcoin is permissible - then so be it. However, if it appears that it is impermissible-then so be it.

We must be careful to not let our own desire to 'get in there quick' when it comes to making money, to move our criteria from 'what is permissible according to Islam (i.e. 'Halal and Haram') to our own selfishly determined 'Benefit and Harm'. Sincerity is to not lie to yourself about the truth. It is a right of Allah, His Divine Book, His Messenger, the Khaleefah and his governors and those of knowledge that sincere advice must be offered in the best manner, and it must be accepted, no matter how it was given. We remind ourselves and those engaged in this area of the statement of Imam al-Hafiz al-Dhahabi about his Shaykh al-Harawi,

"*The Sheikh of Islam is beloved to us, but the Truth is more beloved to us than the Sheikh of Islam!*"

PART 1- ASCERTAINING THE REALITY OF BITCOIN

Before evaluating the Islamic position on a matter, it is important to have correctly ascertained the reality of the issue being investigated. The *manaat* (reality) is defined as the matter to which the Islamic legal ("*shar'i*") rule (the "*hukm*") applies and conforms to. However, it is neither its evidence nor its *'illah* (i.e. the motive behind the rule). Consequently, to establish the *manat* requires an understanding of the non-textual reality within which the Islamic ruling applies. For example, the *shar'i* rule is the prohibition of intoxicants and thus establishing whether a specific drink is an intoxicant, is referred to as establishing the *manat-ul-hukm*. Being a non-textual element, the person establishing the *manat* need not be a *mujtahid* or even Muslim, given that the aim is to ascertain the reality of the matter, and this has nothing to do with knowledge of the *Shariah*, or the Arabic language; the aim is rather confined to cognising the reality.

Therefore, our objective in this part of the paper is simply to establish the manaat regarding Bitcoin. For this purpose, we are not focusing on other cryptocurrencies or Initial Coin Offerings (which is somewhat separate as issues). This is because the reality of cryptocurrencies can vary between themselves and they must be analysed on a case by case basis to a large degree. Here we will only be addressing Bitcoin. It goes without saying that the underlying Blockchain technology is extremely useful and presents many opportunities to be utilised effectively and this is always to be encouraged.

ORIGINS

Bitcoin is the most popular of what has become known as decentralised digital *"cryptocurrencies"*[4]. As a cryptocurrency, it uses cryptography to control its creation and management rather than relying on a central authority (e.g. the Bank of England). It differs from other virtual currencies such as those created by Nike, Vodafone, Amazon and those that are often used in the computer gaming industry for so called "in-game purchases" as, unlike Bitcoins, all of these previous virtual currencies have been centrally controlled and managed.

To start from the beginning, the concept behind Bitcoin originated in an online paper published under the pseudonym Satoshi Nakamoto in November 2008 entitled *Bitcoin: A Peer-to-Peer Electronic Cash System*[5]. The paper proposed a peer-to-peer form of electronic cash which would allow online payments to be sent directly from one party to another without requiring the involvement of a financial institution or third party (e.g. PayPal) (similar, in principle, to the concept of media file-sharing through platforms such as Napster). Instead of placing trust in such third parties and paying the fees associated with their services, Bitcoin requires users to place trust in the protocol that underpins the system which has thus far proved very resilient.

---

[4]   Bitcoin A Primer for Policymakers, 2013, Jerry Brito and Andrea Castillo, George
      Mason University, http://mercatus.org/sites/default/files/Brito_BitcoinPrimer.pdf
[5]   Bitcoin: A Peer-to-Peer Electronic Cash System, Satoshi Nakamoto,
      www.bitcoin.org/bitcoin.pdf

The Bitcoin network came into existence in January 2009 with the release of the first open-source (freely distributable) Bitcoin client software and the issuance of the first 'bitcoins'[6].

BLOCK CHAIN

Every transaction that occurs in the Bitcoin economy is registered in a public ledger (the "**Block Chain**") which is distributed among all the users of the Bitcoin system via a peer-to-peer network. This enables Bitcoin to avoid the issue known in computer science as the "double-spending" problem[7] where, without third party intermediaries, electronic money could, in theory, be spent twice, in the absence of ledgers and records to keep track of electronic money transfers.

The Block Chain is maintained by a network of computers that process the payments of bitcoins (a process called "**Mining**"; the individuals who contribute computer power to this process are called "**Miners**"). In return for their contribution Miners receive newly created bitcoins. Once all bitcoins have been mined, they will instead be able to charge fees ("**Rewards**") for these services.

VALUE OF BITCOIN

Transactions on the Bitcoin network are NOT denominated in real world currency units such as Dollars, Euros or Sterling (as they are on PayPal); nor is the value of the currency derived from gold or government fiat. The Bitcoin price is derived from the subjective value that people assign to it

---

[6]   The Rise and Fall of Bitcoin, 2011, Benjamin Wallace, Wired Magazine,
      http://www.wired.com/magazine/2011/11/mf_bitcoin/

[7]   Achieving Electronic Privacy, 1992, David Chaum,
      http://www.chaum.com/articles/Achieving_Electronic_Privacy.htm

only (and its value relative to real currencies as determined on an open market). Regardless of all of the blockchain technology and other technological innovations behind it, Bitcoin has no intrinsic value of its own. Its value derives solely from the confidence in the market. Blockchain technology is ofcourse hugely valuable however it must be separated from Bitcoin as Bitcoin is a 'product'which simply uses this technology. They are not the same and should not be confused. Despite Bitcoin's lack of any intrinsic value, its market price bounces around between $15,000 and $20,000 (or some other number depending on when you're reading this in the world). The difference is pure stock market speculation – one person's bet that another person will be willing to buy that Bitcoin for more than the first person paid for it.

We will return to consider the issue of value later as this ties in to the requirements of assets and currencies from an Islamic perspective.

TRANSACTIONS AND PAYMENT PROCESSING

Transactions are verified through the use of public-key cryptography. Public-key cryptography requires that each user be assigned two "keys", one private key that is kept secret like a password, and one public key that can be shared with the world. The public and private keys are stored in an individual's "Wallet" which can exist in both physical and digital forms.

When an individual ("A") wishes to transfer bitcoins to another individual ("B"), A creates a message (a "Transaction") containing B's public key and signing off with A's private key. The Transaction is then recorded, time stamped and displayed in one "block" of the Block Chain as part of the payment processing carried out by Miners.

Each time a transaction is made it must be verified by a Miner prior to the recipient's funds being cleared. In order to do so, an active computer on the Bitcoin network must assign a "hash key" to the block (a randomly generated value that describes the entire block). This hash key is then transmitted to the rest of the network and is used to confirm that the Transaction in the given block is legitimate and that the funds can be cleared. The process results in a 10-60 minute delay in clearing of funds but it also means there is no need for a central payments processing system.

Therefore, Bitcoins are basically just numbers and the process of mining is the process of generating numbers.

ADVANTAGES

Lower transaction costs

The removal of third-party intermediaries makes Bitcoin transactions substantially cheaper and quicker than traditional payment networks. This is particularly attractive to small businesses that are seeking to lower transaction costs. For example, although credit cards have made it easier to do business, this is at a considerable cost to merchants. In addition, credit card payments are susceptible to fraudulent charge-backs (or consumer-initiated payment reversals) based on false claims that a product has not been delivered[8]. However, credit cards do afford some protection for users the removal of which may have a detrimental effect on business. From our research, Bitcoin currently does not have such forms of protection; however, businesses could emerge offering such services as the provision of escrow arrangements, amongst others.

Inflation

The lack of control over inflation has been a significant concern for many in relation to the adoption of Bitcoin. Inflation may be influenced by supply of and demand for a currency. However, Inflation can not be affected by the manipulation of the supply of bitcoins as the Bitcoin system was designed to mimic the extraction of gold or other precious metals from the Earth in the sense that only a limited amount can ever be mined. Written into the protocol of Bitcoin is an upper limit of 21 million bitcoins (Note – each bitcoin has 100,000,000 sub-units called "Satoshi"). As the Bitcoin

---

[8]   Emily Maltby, "Chargebacks Create Business Headaches," Wall Street Journal, February 10, 2011,
http://online.wsj.com/article/SB10001424052748704698004576104554234202010
.html

limit is approached, the Rewards for mining bitcoins will reduce in a series of steps occurring approximately every four years to compensate for an increase in total processing power (once the limit is reached transaction fees will be introduced). As such, the rate of expansion of the currency is prescribed and should plateau by around 2030. The de-centralised nature of the currency, the prescribed rate of growth and the upper limit all mean it is impossible for any single person or entity to increase the supply of Bitcoins.

Inflation may occur if demand is significantly reduced. However, as Bitcoin is a distributed system of currency, if demand were to decrease to such an extent as to cause inflation then the system itself would fail in any case[9]. If Bitcoin continues to be adopted and eventually becomes a mainstream unit of 'currency' adopted by states then this is unlikely to be of any concern.

Potential to combat poverty and oppression

Access to basic financial services is a significant hindrance to combating poverty. Due to the impediments to developing traditional branch banking in under-developed areas, people in developing countries have turned to mobile banking services for their financial needs. Bitcoin is able to provide people in developing counties with inexpensive access to financial services on a global scale. This is beginning to be seen in countries such as Kenya, Tanzania and Afghanistan, where the closed-system mobile payment service M-Pesa has been particularly successful.

Bitcoin may also be able to provide relief to countries with strict capital controls as there is no central authority that can reverse transactions or

---

[9]   Bitcoin wiki: Myths, 29 December 2013,
      https://en.bitcoin.it/wiki/Myths#Bitcoin_can.27t_work_because_there_is_no_way_t
      o_control_inflation

prevent the exchange of bitcoins between countries. Bitcoin therefore provides an alternative in countries with devalued currencies or frozen capital markets. Individuals in oppressive or emergency situations might also benefit from the privacy that Bitcoin can provide.

CHALLENGES

Volatility

The value of bitcoins has fluctuated dramatically in the last few years in what has closely resembled traditional speculative 'bubbles'. Over-optimistic media coverage of Bitcoin prompts the participation of novice investors which pushes up the value of Bitcoins, until it is over-valued and, as a result, subsequently drops, losing significant amounts of money in the process.[10]

Bitcoin's volatility has divided opinion as to whether the system is a viable alternative to real world currencies. It has been suggested that the speculative bubbles seen to date are simply fluctuations that are stress testing the 'currency' and will decrease in frequency.[11] It is also possible that volatility will decrease as users become more familiar with the Bitcoin technology and develop realistic expectations about its future. However, despite the amount of time that has passed, there shows little sign of stability unless Bitcoin is accepted as an everyday monetary medium by states as opposed to an asset reflecting an investment opportunity (we discuss this in more detail below).

Periods of high volatility are not uncommon in current world currencies and asset classes, particularly in commodities and emerging markets. Howecer, Bitcoin's volatility is extreme, and frequent: the one-day price move has been more than 10 percent on nine days in the past three months and the run-up to the new year of 2018 has shown a massive drop in the

---

[10] Felix Salmon, "The Bitcoin Bubble and the Future of Currency," Medium, April 3, 2013, https://medium.com/money-banking/2b5ef79482cb

[11] Adam Gurri, "Bitcoins, Free Banking, and the Optional Clause," Ümlaut, May 6, 2013, http://theumlaut.com/2013/05/06/bitcoins-free-banking-and-the-optional-clause/

value of Bitcoin with it losing over a third of its value in 24 hours[12] and its fluctuation on certain days having gone to as much as 45 per cent less.[13]

Tim Swanson, a bitcoin expert and founder of Post Oak Labs, a technology advisory firm, said he was concerned that if the futures liquidity increases there could be an incentive for someone with a large bet against bitcoin to disrupt or attack the network to make money from the ensuing price fall.[14] Indeed recent weeks suggest that we are already seeing a dip in the 'value' of Bitcoin generally!

Security

The Bitcoin protocol has thus far proved to be impervious to hacking; the majority of challenges instead concern Wallet services and bitcoin exchanges[15]. However, if users are not careful they can inadvertently delete or misplace bitcoins and, as with cash, once lost it cannot be recovered. Further, if users do not protect their private addresses then they leave themselves open to theft. Bitcoin Wallets can now be secured by means of encryption; however, users must choose to activate the encryption. Failure to do so could result in bitcoins being stolen through malware. The media has also reported on several attacks on Bitcoin exchanges which have resulted in thefts or downtime of services as a result of distributed denial-of-service ("DDoS") attacks. Many of the security risks facing Bitcoin are

---

[12] http://money.cnn.com/2017/12/22/investing/bitcoin-plunges-below-14k/index.html

[13] http://uk.businessinsider.com/bitcoin-price-drops-plunges-friday-december-22-2017-12?r=US&IR=T

[14] https://uk.reuters.com/article/uk-markets-bitcoin-risks-insight/bitcoin-fever-exposes-crypto-market-frailties-idUKKBN1E724X

[15] Dan Kaminsky, "I Tried Hacking Bitcoin and I Failed," Business Insider, April 12, 2013, http://www.businessinsider.com/dan-kaminsky-highlights-flaws-bitcoin-2013-4

similar to those facing real world currencies; bank notes can be destroyed or lost and banks can be robbed or targeted by DDoS attacks.

Criminal use

A significant concern in relation to Bitcoin has been the anonymity of the system. In the absence of third-parties, Transactions take place only between two individuals and, as is the case when paying for items and services in cash; no record is explicitly made of the individuals involved. The public keys used in transactions are recorded but these are not currently tied to anyone's identity. However, in the sense that all transactions to and from a particular Bitcoin address can be traced, it is more accurate to describe Bitcoin as pseudonymous rather that anonymous.

A concern that results from this lack of a tie between virtual and real-world identities is that Bitcoin may be used for the purposes of money laundering, financing terrorism and trafficking of illegal goods. However, the public record of all Bitcoin transactions contained in the public ledger allows for the ongoing tracing of funds through transactions and so until such time as a public key is matched with a real world identity, any misused funds can be traced and followed.

Some exchanges have already taken steps to comply with anti-money laundering, record-keeping and reporting requirements[16]. This, combined with the public ledger will go some way towards reducing the risk that bitcoins will be used for such purposes. It is also important to note that

---

[16] Jeffrey Sparshott, "Bitcoin Exchange Makes Apparent Move to Play by U.S. Money-Laundering Rules," Wall Street Journal, June 28, 2013, http://online.wsj.com/article/SB10001424127887323873904578574000957464468.html

many of the potential downsides associated with the potential criminal use of bitcoins are similar to those facing traditional cash.

Nonetheless, there still exists structural designs within Bitcoin's framework that allow the mixing of 'clean' and 'dirty' money. There exists the use of so-called "tumblers" to mix illegally obtained funds with "clean" funds, the intention being to confuse the trail back to the fund's original source. These services are available on the internet, with one provider having the audacity to call its website "bitlaunder.com".

Importantly, the pseudonymous nature of Bitcoin means those who own the largest amounts of Bitcoin (termed as "Whales") cannot be identified and that those who mine it also benefit from the same. This is extremely dangerous given the affect that they can cause to the 'value' should they decide to act ns any particular direction with respect to their holdings. This 'unknown' element is an important consideration also form an Islamic legal standpoint and we shall revisit this when we discuss the concept of *majhool* (i.e. unknown) in Islamic law especially because it goes right to the core of Bitcoin's design as being something which is being issued by an 'unknown' entity.

Scalability and splinters in Bitcoin versions

The security of Bitcoin is generally accepted. However, it comes at the cost of a 'daily transaction limit' to Bitcoin payments. In the original Bitcoin design, each component ("**block**") in the Blockchain is used to store transactions made by the users as well as the other sensitive information. So a block can store multiple transactions but this must be within the specified size limit of 1MB. Whenever a block is completed, it is added to the Blockchain as a permanent record. As a matter of fact, this 1MB block size limit was imposed to prevent the Blockchain from the potential DDoS attacks by the hackers who might try to freeze the network by creating blocks of uneven or massive size. But as long as the size limit is as low as 1MB, all the blocks exceeding this size will be automatically rejected by the network and they will not be added to the Blockchain.[17] This limit is a design element of Bitcoin alone, as opposed to the underlying Blockchain technology, and its implementation is a crucial security measure that comprises part of the state of the Bitcoin network. As such, it suggests that the original Bitcoin protocol itself did not contemplate accommodating a massive user base in the same way currencies do. A surge in bitcoin trades in recent weeks has also left the blockchain network that the cryptocurrency relies on to process and verify transactions struggling to keep up. As of Wednesday 13 December 2017, at 14.45 GMT, more than 125,000 bitcoin transactions remained unconfirmed.

In order to solve the issue of the transaction limit (which caused a raging debate between 'Bitcoin Believers') Bitcoin actually splintered into two versions of the currency in August 2017 (known as the "hard fork"). The original product is now known as 'legacy Bitcoin' and the new version is known as 'Bitcoin Cash'.[18] Legacy Bitcoin's blocks are capped at 1MB, and Bitcoin Cash can support up to 8MB (with current blocks having 2MB). Bigger block sizes is the major difference between the two and the impetus for the split. However, it has been noted that Bitcoin is looking increasingly likely to splinter off again, creating a third version known as 'SegWit' as miners and developers pursue separate visions to scale its rapidly growing marketplace. There exists an ongoing debate between 'Bitcoin Believers' as

---

[17] https://www.quora.com/What-is-block-size-limit-with-regard-to-bitcoin-and-blockchain

[18] http://www.gambling911.com/businessfinancial/coingeek-interviews-bitcoin-evangelist-roger-ver-.html

regards to conception of the Bitcoin system – which was designed around scarcity and whose traditionalists insist on keeping the block size small in order to maintain security etc. It is clear that it was never actually designed to be a particularly convenient means of payment for the masses to go an buy their groceries.[19]

---

[19] https://www.bloomberg.com/view/articles/2017-11-14/bitcoin-s-high-transaction-fees-show-its-limits

SO IS IT A CURRENCY OR AN ASSET?

It is clear that Bitcoin (whichever version you are referring to) has carved out a disruptive place in the capital markets. The reality of the product is causing debate in all spheres of academia and industry. NYU Professor Aswath Damodoran, has staked his claim that Bitcoin is officially a "currency" not an "asset" as so many others claim. He defines assets as something that generates cash now or is expected to generate cash in the future. Currently the only way to generate cash from Bitcoin is by selling some that you already own. In contrast, Initial Coin Offerings (ICOs) or equity offerings of startups priced in cryptocurrencies, would be construed as an asset because the coin-holder theoretically has a claim on the future cash flows of the business (but these are not being considered in this paper).

However, Damodaran fails to effectively define what a currency is beyond a 'medium of exchange'. Those who term Bitcoin as falling into the relams of an 'asset' do so on the basis of two key observations: 1) its value being unstable and 2) its transaction processing is too slow.

We have addressed the issue of the transaction limit above (see section: *Scalability and splinters in Bitcoin versions*) aswell as addressing the idea of how the value of Bitcoin is determined (see section: *Value of Bitcoins*) and how it is extremely volatile (see section: *Volatility*).

Stability and Liquidity as conditions for currencies

A key feature of a currency is that it be a stable store of value.[20] Too high a level of instability in currency values mean that people cannot trade or finance their economic activity and investors cannot accurately predict the

---

value of future earnings. Currently, it is clear that currencies are not expected to function so as to be capable of losing half their value in a few months (such as Bitcoin recently did). Bitcoin is considered a highly volatile currency and it must be made clear that as much as it can go up in price, Bitcoin also has the potential to lose significant value, fast.[21] Such volatility is characteristic of 'assets' such as publically listed shares on stock exchanges and other financial instruments. The 2017 current record-breaking rise in Bitcoin's 'value' on the markets has only furthered fears of an impending crash or at the very least a correction with the drop in price in December 2017 has increasing and indicating these concerns further. Indeed the hundred-fold increase in its price has strengthened arguments of those who argue it should be understood as an asset.

A further role of currencies is that they facilitate transactions. As mentioned in the section relating to the issues of Bitcoin's scalability, the framework of Bitcoin itself is not designed to actually function as an alternative currency for the masses. The very nature and security of Bitcoin means that it suffers from the same problems the normal Barter system does, whereby it is hard to make changes and you must find two people who want to exchange goods (three or four way trades get complicated). Whilst this is fine to do in the case of large scale corporate and capital markets transactions (for example, PwC Hong Kong has recently in 2017 accepted Bitcoin as payment of a real estate related transaction), to protect the security of the Blockchain that makes cryptocurrencies like Bitcoin so secure, processing of Bitcoin transactions is very slow. We argue that to change these rules will compromise the current security of the system and therefore it is tenuous to argue that Bitcoin can become a widely-used currency. Its very security negates its value in everyday use as its decentralised nature means that it

---

[21] https://www.luno.com/blog/en/post/bitcoin-and-islam

cannot provide the stability needed to facilitate transactions widely (atleast not at the time of writing).

In terms of its treatment generally, compared with fiat currency, Bitcoin is being treated more akin to a financial instrument. The Norwegian government has subjected it to capital gains tax.[22] The U.S. Securities Exchange Commision has recently laid out guidelines with respect to its treatment as a financial instrument consitituting a 'security' for the purposes of being a regulated product. The Internal Revenue Service has also ruled that Bitcoin and other "convertible virtual currencies" are "treated as property" and not treated as currency.[23]

A further point to consider is that of Regulation. Bitcoin's decentralised nature means that it does not fall under the jurisdiction or responsibility of any one state. There is no formal regulatory body. This makes it hard to address Bitcoin-related fraud cases. This is not the case with traditional currencies. Law looks at both substance and form. The regulatory approach varies across jurisdictions with many not regulating crytpocurrencies per se, as these are not considered as 'securities' or 'legal tender', but rather regulating the exchange process as a money service business. The U.S. regulates exchanges and administrators as subject to the Bank Secrecy Act, whilst users are covered by tax legislation as virtual currencies are generally treated as property with gains or losses calculated. The Hong Kong Monetary Authority does not regulate it and the Monetary Authority of Singapore is undergoing a consultation process as a precursor for introducing regulation. Whilst, there are jurisdictions which do not yet

---

[22] http://coinalert.eu/2015013940-Breaking+News-+Norway+Doesn-t+Consider+Bitcoin+a+Legitimate+Currency.html

[23] https://www.thebalance.com/how-bitcoins-are-taxed-3192871

classify Bitcoin as a security and therefore regulate it in this way, the U.S. Financial Crimes Enforcement Network defines such currencies as "*A medium of exchange that operates like a currency in some environments, but does not have all the attributes of real currency.*" From our research, Bitcoin does not have 'legal tender' status in any jurisdiction.

The reality of Bitcoin is that you can create the populace is capable of creating its own currency. Government treasuries are usually responsible for the creation of currency but with Bitcoin you can actually create currency yourself if you have enough computing power.

Based on my research to date and the discussions I have had with those far more knowledgeable than mysef, I can only conclude that Bitcoin is to be considered an asset and not a currency. In this regard, I go further to say that it can only be considered a 'virtual asset' and not a 'real asset' as a result of the lack of an inherent intrinsic value to it. There is little evidence to suggest that buyers are using bitcoin as a means of exchange and payment. On the whole, they buy the cryptocurrency as a speculative investment, attracted by massive price gains.[24]

So in conclusion, despite claims to be a 'virtual currency', Bitcoin is simply a 'virtual asset' for the simple reason that:

> "*If it looks like a duck and sounds like a duck, it usually is.*"[25]

---

[24] Garrick Hileman, a research fellow at the University of Cambridge's Judge Business School.

[25] https://www.gtreview.com/news/fintech/icos-the-next-goldmine-for-trade-finance-lenders/?utm_medium=email&utm_campaign=GTR%20eNews&utm_content=GTR%20eNews+CID_b7c69a50e13f74a02d91c586d70c2d74&utm_source=Email%20marketing%20software

PART 2 - THE ISLAMIC PERSPECTIVE ON BITCOIN

Above, we have aimed to establish the reality of what Bitcoin is. Below we shall assess the Islamic principles and legal considerations which apply to it. Notwithstanding that we have concluded above that Bitcoin is an asset and not a currency, for completeness, we will evaluate Bitcoin through the use of both the laws relating to currencies and those to assets as litmus tests.

IS BITCOIN A CURRENCY ACCORDING TO ISLAM?

What qualifies as a currency from Islam? In defining a 'currency', it is clear that a 'currency' is defined as "*a recognised specific unit of exchange, which is the basis to which goods and labour are related and by which they are measured.*"

A State 'coins' and 'mints' currency which it adopts in a specific form and fashion (with a specified weight and value). The value can be based on a standard such as the 'bi-metallic standard', 'representative money standard' (in both of these the value derives from an actual commodity) or another standard such as the fiat standard adopted by states today (where the value is simply established by government decree).

Some have argued that Bitcoin is to be treated as currency even though it has no intrinsic value (i.e. being linked to a commodity) because the same applies to fiat currency. However, this misses the point of what a currency is as the sharing of one or two common features with fiat currency (in terms of it not being backed by a commodity) or even with gold and silver (in that it must be Mined), does not mean that Bitcoin fulfils all the conditions of what a currency is.

These 'conditions' of what constitutes a currency, as laid out by Ustadh Abu Khalid, are observable in reality as applying to all currencies:[26]

1)   It acts as a basis to evaluate the goods & services, i.e it is a measure for prices and wages (as mentioned above);

2)   It is issued by a central authority, not an unknown body (*majhool*), which undertakes the responsibility of issuing the currency;

3)   It is widespread and easily accessible to the people and it is not exclusive to a group of people only.

So does Bitcoin meet these conditons? Some argue that it is possible that Bitcoin could reach a stage in popular usage whereby it becomes a genuine basis to evaluate goods & services in the future and thereby satisfies condition 1 of being a currency (mentioned above). This is not currently the case as during a particularly volatile period of trading on 7 December 2017, Bitcoin surged from below $16,000 to $19,500 in less than an hour on Coinbase's Global Digital Asset Exchange (GDAX), while it was changing hands at less than $16,000 on another, Bitstamp.

Argument are also made that it is possible that in the future it could become more accessible and thereby meet condition 3 too. However, in this regard, we refer them to Part 1 of this paper we discussed the issues of Scalability. Importantly in respect of accesibility, on the 13 December 2017, Reuters reported that Coinbase (one of the biggest providers of digital currency wallets) went down under the weight of heavy traffic leaving many of its more than 10 million customers unable to access their funds. It is important to remember that some of the largest holders of Bitcoin are unknown and

---

[26]   http://islamicsystem.blogspot.com.es/2017/06/the-reality-of-cryptocurrencies-such-as.html

include private individuals. As such, whatever action these entities choose to take will have a huge impact on the value of Bitcoin at any point in time.

Based on the above considerations, it is clear that the volatility of Bitcoin, the way in which it is priced (based on speculation of the market) and the lack of an intrinsic value of any sort mean that it is not something that can meet the reason of 'ease for the people in pricing and transacting'. Alongside what we have mentioned of the reality of Bitcoin, the fact that its 'value' can change so dramatically within the time it takes to complete a transaction is itself indicative of this.

Bitcoin and Gold

Some have tried to present an equivalence between Bitcoin and other things such as fiat currencies, gold, tulips etc. However, whilst there are some similarities between Bitcoin and these, the differences far outweigh the similarities.

In the case of Gold, the argument made is that both can be mined. However, this ignores the reality that gold itself is different in its capacity as an asset from its capacity as a currency. You can mine gold but it would only be an asset and only once minted by the currency-issuing authority would it constitute currency. From an Islamic perspective, we need only consider the Zakat rules applicable to gold as an asset which do not apply to it as a currency. Similarly, in the case of Bitcoin, the mere existence of it and calling it a currency (and equating it to gold) does not make it so from a legal standpoint. In addition, mining Bitcoin is very different from mining gold. Gold's intrinsic value goes well beyond its minability, as it is desirable for many other reasons outside of its market value. Gold experienced a frenzy of buying that drove its price up to $1,900 in 2011 and was described as a bubble, which burst in 2012, but the price remained above $1,000 with trading over a relatively narrow range since then. Gold is valued as jewelry throughout the world and is further supported at lower prices as an industrial commodity. Bitcoin, on the other hand has no such value, and its price could rise to any figure, even a million dollars, or it could just as easily plummet to a few cents.[27]

Therefore, those who equate them should be mindful of drawing a false comparison between dissimilar things as it is an example of false equivalence fallacy.

---

[27] http://www.khilafah.com/bitcoin-the-mother-of-all-bubbles/

THE NEED FOR A CENTRALISED AUTHORITY AND UNDERSTANDING THE 'UNKNOWN'

Ustadh Abu Khaled, Sheikh Ata and Mufti Faraz discuss this issue in their publications. Notably they reach different conclusions. However, it is clear in both of their works that there is a general view amongst Islamic jurists that there must be a central authority (with detailed discussion of this in the Shafi' school and by the likes of Ibn Khaldun).

Mufti Faraz focuses on the condition regarding the need for a centralised issuing authority and states that Islamic legal opinions show that jurists favoured a centralised monetary system because of the following reasons:[28]

1)   Trust in the currency
2)   Presence of a regulatory framework
3)   Secure system
4)   Wide acceptance
5)   Ease for the people in pricing and transacting
6)   A benchmark for transactions.

If one holds the view that a centralised system is necessary for currency, then Bitcoin falls short of this and cannot be considered a currency. If one views that a decentralised system is permitted (assuming it achieves the same aims of a centralised system), then an argument can be made that Bitcoin is a currency. However, such an argument seems tenous when we consider reason 5 of those mentioned above and also when we consider the nature of the decentralised authority in question.

---

[28]   https://afinanceorg.files.wordpress.com/2017/08/research-paper-on-bitcoin-mufti-faraz-adam.pdf

Whilst Mufti Faraz presents well the arguement that a decentralised authority is possible, we favour the majority argument that a centralised authority is needed for the issuing of currency according to Islamic law.

In traditional fiat currencies, 'agreement' on the question of which coins exist is achieved by fiat, as their name suggests: some central authority issues coins and is the final arbiter of the validity of coins. The money is allocated to the appropriate purse by a central authority through a hierarchy of delegated powers (for example, the Bank of England allows recognised banks to represent money as mere annotations in bookkeeping systems, and banks, in turn, allow me to write cheques, which cause these annotations to change) [29] In the case of Bitcoin, however, we are talking about a 'decentralised system'. In this case, there can be no central authority to defer to. Instead we must have 'agreement' (or consensus) amongst some group. Group consensus is a well-studied problem and can be arrived at in many ways, but in essence all solutions are the same: consensus is arrived at when some sufficient number of members of the group agree. For example, we could say that consensus is arrived at when more than half the members agree, and this would work, since the remaining members cannot change the consensus. However, in the cases of currency, to match this to the notion of 'decentralised' (i.e. lacking central authority) the consensus group must be, at least, all participants in the currency. This does not present any real problem when that group is known. For example, it would be possible to define the group as "all people currently in the United Kingdom" – where the currency would be something akin to the Pound Sterling. Assuming the majority decide to behave honestly, then they should have no difficulty in forming consensus on who has how much money at what time. However, the actual notion of decentralisation does not admit such restrictions. After

---

[29] http://www.links.org/files/decentralised-currencies.pdf

all, in some sense, placing any such restriction simply pushes the central authority back a layer - instead of controlling the currency, the authority controls membership of the consensus group.[30] A system like this must allow any entity to participate, and to join and leave the scheme at will and it is here where the problem lies. If you can never know who is in the scheme, then you can never get agreement. Given Bitcoin is not issued by a central authority which undertakes responsibility for its issuance, the source of Bitcoins generation remains 'unknown'. Bitcoin can be issued by anyone who has the relevant mining software and a computer with an internet connection (you also require a pretty powerful computer and this costs alot of electricity!). It is therefore reliant on the honesty on the part of and trust placed in this unknown 'community' of miners who, in turn for those willing to pay for the service, mine Bitcoins. As to why the community is unknown, this is because whilst one particular miner is identifiable, it is impossible to identify the 'community' as a whole. As a result of this, the community is 'unknown' (ie. *majhool*) as an entity.

The Islamic view towards the issuance of currency is that the issuing entity cannot be unknown. This forms the basis of the requirement for a centralised authority. From our research, the issuance of currency is the responsibility of this authority and no individual or group of individuals can have the right to issue currency even if they possess the means and styles to be able to do so, because this would lead to havoc and anarchy among the masses. For example, even if people possess gold and silver, they cannot convert it into currency themselves. Instead they will have to buy the currency in return for their gold and silver. The authority undertakes the responsibility of issuing the currency (e.g. dirhams and dinars).

---

[30] http://www.links.org/files/decentralised-currencies.pdf

The juristic principle in play here is:

ما لا يتم الواجب الا به فهو واجب

"*Whatever a wajib cannot be completed without, then that is also wajib.*"

A centralised system is necessary given that, as we discussed in detail in Part 1 of this paper, the currency must be capable of facilitating transactions generally within society. Having a decentralised authority, in particular one which is 'unknown', works against this principle aswell as against the ideas of having stable value and access.

The very nature and security of Bitcoin means that it suffers from the same problems the normal Barter system whereby it is hard to make changes and you must find two people who want to exchange goods (three or four way trades get complicated). To protect the security of the Blockchain that makes cryptocurrencies like Bitcoin so secure, processing of Bitcoin transactions is very slow. In fact, because of a limit on the number of transactions which can be completed in a day, it sometimes takes days to complete a simple transaction.[31] To change these rules will compromise the current security of the system and therefore it is tenuous to argue that Bitcoin can become a widely-used currency. Its very security negates its value in everyday use as its decentralised nature means that it cannot provide the stability needed to facilitate transactions widely.

We note the argument presented by Mufti Faraz regarding the possibility of Bitcoin to become currency through accepted customary usage (*Ta'amul*). However, Mufti Faraz seems to note through his analysis, as do we in ours,

---

[31]   https://www.forbes.com/sites/jeffreydorfman/2017/05/17/bitcoin-is-an-asset-not-a-currency/

that the reality of Bitcoin is such that the argument that Bitcoin can become currency is inconsequential as a result of the nature of it.

In conclusion, in terms of things that can qualify as money, Islam supports intrinsic commodities that can be used as money. Paper or electronic money can also be used but they should be backed by an intrinsic commodity. So is Bitcoin money then? Given that Islam has only recognised commodities of intrinsic value as money including things like gold (Dinar), silver (Dirham); rice, dates, wheat, barley and salt; "*in a strict interpretation of what qualifies as money, Bitcoin probably misses the mark.*"[32]

---

[32]   https://cointelegraph.com/news/is-bitcoin-halal-how-cryptocurrency-conforms-with-islam-and-sharia

SO DOES BITCOIN EVEN QUALIFY AS 'PROPERTY' IN ISLAM?

It is clear that consumers today consider Bitcoin as 'Property' capable of trade and investment (notwithstanding the above discussion as to whether or not it constitutes an asset or currency in real terms). However, is this actually correct to say about Bitcoin from an Islamic perspective?

Defining Property (*Mal*):

In Islamic law, things have linguistic (*lughawi*) and then legal (*shari*) meanings. It is important to therefore define words before using them. In addition there also exist definitions of words established through particular usage and customs (*istilaahi*) which should also be borne in mind. We will here only focus on legal meanings but will give the definition of *Mal* from both perspectives to help illustrate the differences that exist.

Mal (Property) in the Arabic language signifies whatever in effect one may acquire and possess; whether that is corporeal (*`ayn*) or usufruct (*manfa`ah*). Examples include gold, silver, animals, plant and benefit gained out of things such as the riding of vehicles, the wearing of clothes and the residing in houses etc. On the other hand, whatever a man cannot possess, cannot linguistically be regarded as *Mal* - such that generally birds still in the sky, fish in the water, trees in the forest, and minerals in the depths of the earth are not linguistically considered *Mal*.

<u>List of the characteristics which qualify things as *Mal*:</u>

We can summarise as follows that in order for a thing to qualify as Mal it:
1. It has to be naturally desired by man. In modern terminology, it must have 'commercial value'
2. It must be capable of being owned and possessed

3. It must be capable of being stored
4. It must be beneficial in the eyes of the Shariah
5. The ownership of the thing must be assignable and transferable.

A detailed discussion of each of these can be found in the work of Wohidul Islam (1999) and is also touched upon by Mufti Faraz in his paper.

Bitcoin and its uncertain nature (*Gharar*)

Gharar is one of the most strictly prohibited elements in Islamic financial contracts and transactions. Linguistically, the verb *gharra* is the past tense of the noun *gharar*. As a result, gharar is translated as "to mislead, to deceive"[33] In an Islamic legal sense, with regards to financial and commercial contracts, gharar is treated as excessive risk, uncertainty and speculation. Gharar, when defined as 'uncertainty', means the non-existence or unknown nature of the contract's subject matter.

The *ijtihad*s of Ustadh Abu Khaled and Shiekh Ata, aswell as the decision of the Malaysian fatwa council, have stated that Bitcoin is not suitable to be used as currency because there is an element of extreme speculation and uncertainty (*Gharar*) and lack of authoritative body issuing it.[34] It is apparent through an observation of the reality and the Islamic legal provisions relating to Gambling (*Maysir*) and Gharar that Bitcoin possesses the elements of being speculative in terms of its value and that it is traded in a manner akin to gambling. On 14 December 2017, Andrew Bailey (Head of the Financial Conduct Authority) stated that dealing in Bitcoin

---

[33] Baalbaki, R. (2005), Al-Mawrid Al-Quareeb Arabic-English Dictionary. 16th ed. Beirut, Lebanon: Dar El-Ilm Lilmalayin.) p.292

[34] https://www.coingecko.com/buzz/bitcoin-islam-islamic-banking-finance

was 'similar to gambling'. The head of the Central Bank of Australia, Philip Lowe, described the dealing in Bitcoin as 'speculative mania'.[35]

It is narrated by Muslim in his Sahih from Abu Huraira that he said:

نَهَى رَسُولُ اللهِ صلى الله عليه وسلم عَنْ بَيْعِ الْحَصَاةِ، وَعَنْ بَيْعِ الْغَرَرِ

"The Messenger of Allah (ﷺ) forbade Gharar transactions and Hasah transactions."

It is also narrated by Tirmidhi in a hadith from Abu Huraira also:

وَمِنْ بُيُوعِ الْغَرَرِ بَيْعُ السَّمَكِ فِي الْمَاءِ وَبَيْعُ الْعَبْدِ الْآبِقِ وَبَيْعُ الطَّيْرِ فِي السَّمَاءِ وَنَحْوُ ذَلِكَ مِنَ الْبُيُوعِ

"The Gharar sale includes selling fish that are in the water, selling a slave that has escaped, selling birds that are in the sky and similar type of sales all of which are prohibited."

In this regard it is apparent that the ambiguous and unknown (i.e. *majhool* and *ghayr ma'loom*) fall to also be things which are Gharar.

---

[35]   https://www-bbc-com.cdn.ampproject.org/c/s/www.bbc.com/news/amp/business-42360553

Does Bitcoin have 'Utility' and 'Value' in the *Shariah*'s eyes?

When considering this issue, we must make a distinction between what is necessary for an asset to be considered as having 'value' versus that for a currency. Fiat currencies, even though not backed by an asset, still derive their 'value' from the power of the states who issue them and who use them as currency. As such, they are deemed to have 'utility' and 'value'. However, for a commodity to be classified as an asset, it has to have 'utility' innately as it is from this utility that the commodity derives its 'value' in the first place. The 'utility' here is not defined based on subjective terms but rather it is studied objectively.

What is the value? The value is the amount of benefit present within the commodity, which is fixed at all times and places. So the benefit of a jug is estimated, in itself as an object, by the materials it is made of, its suitability for carrying water, whether for drinking or ablution. These uses are never detached of it today or tomorrow, whether its price increased or declined.[36]

For example, a loaf of bread has utility and provides clear benefit to its holder for consumption. The same goes for a house as a person who possesses the house can live in it, rent it and so on. So the loaf and the house are both considered assets in this case and therefore are *Mal* from the *shari'* standpoint. In contrast, the mud on your shoes has no utility and therefore no value despite the fact that mud may be of value to someone who wants to build a mud house. It is important to note here that utility is 'objectively' determined as if we are using a 'subjective' basis then literally everything can have some 'utility' and 'value' to someone, somewhere!

---

[36] http://islamicsystem.blogspot.co.uk/2012/06/q-difference-between-value-and-price-by.html

Therefore, Bitcoin does not fulfill the conditions of an asset because it has no 'utility' innately whatsoever (this is of course not the case with the Blockchain technology- which has huge potential) and is currently only being ascribed its 'utility' by those who call for it to be used as a currency and those who barter using it.

When looking at this from an Islamic legal sense and the reality, we must remember that we have accepted that Bitcoin is not a currency and therefore it is incorrect to 'ascribe' value to Bitcoin in the way a currency can be 'ascribed' value. This is because if we accept Bitcoin as an asset, and agree that something can only be regarded as an asset based on its utility and not on the ability to sell it or buy it or sell using it to a subjective class, then it is clear that Bitcoin does not have this innate utility and is only ascribed it.

The buyer of Bitcoins cannot utilise it in any manner except that he sells it or barters it with those who also ascribe value to it. However, of course the *Shariah* prohibits the selling of something that does not have any objective utility and resultant 'value' and this is why Bitcoin cannot be considered as a commercial asset. Therefore, Bitcoin, whilst of course being something that exists as a 'virtual asset', is not Mal (property) in Islam because of the fact that it has no utility innately (which is a condition for assets in Islam), the unknown nature of its source and due to the Gharar in it. The only utility that Bitcoin has is ascribed utility that emanates from the ascribed speculative value that people give it, but this ascribing of utility and value is something that can only be done with currencies and not assets. As Bitcoin is not a currency, the ascribed utility it has is worthless and this is what leads to many to call Bitcoin 'nothing'. As for the evidence for an asset to have value, this is established through the conditions of what constitutes *Mal* (as an asset is in of itself a category of *Mal*) and has been discussed in the books of Fiqh.

PART 3- CONCLUSION

In conclusion, in establishing the *Manat* (reality) of Bitcoin, it is clear that this falls to be considered in the realm of 'assets' and not actual 'currency' in both reality and according to Islamic law.[37]

When considering both the laws applicable to currencies and those applicable to assets, we see that Bitcoin does not fulfil the conditions that Islam lays out.

As a 'currency' it fails to meet the requirements to be a stable store of value, a benchmark by which people can trade aswell as being produced by a central authority that can provide such stability and access to the masses. Indeed through an observation of the reality, we can see that it was not actually designed in a manner that facilitates en masse transactions. The current splinters and security concerns being raised regarding it are testament to this.

As an 'asset' it fails to meet the requirements to be free from Gharar and is issued by a Majhool source (a mining community). It lacks any intrinsic value and any value that attaches to it is merely as a result of pure extreme speculation (Maysir).

---

[37]   https://afinanceorg.files.wordpress.com/2017/08/research-paper-on-bitcoin-mufti-faraz-adam.pdf

1. Therefore, Bitcoin is a thing that is forbidden to deal in. It falls into the first of three kinds of products that cannot be dealt in by Muslims. These are:

2. Products which are forbidden in and of themselves;

3. Products which are acquired through force or theft; and

4. Products which are permissible in origin but are acquired through an illegal means.

Bitcoin falls into the first of these categories because it is forbidden specifically for itself (like alcohol). It is therefore forbidden to be given as a gift, or to be borrowed, or sold, or bought in the same way that it is forbidden for the person who gives the alcohol, and is forbidden for the person it is gifted to, or the one who sells it, or buys it or the one who borrows it. The Messenger (ﷺ) said:

حُرِّمَتِ الْخَمْرُ بِعَيْنِهَا

"Alcohol is forbidden for itself"   [Narrated by Nisa'i]

In the case of Bitcoin, it falls into the first category as it is plagued with Gharar, Maysir and its source is majhool and it is clear that it is merely a 'virtual asset' and a product which lacks intrinsic value. As narrated by Nafi (ra) reported from Umar (ra) that the Prophet (ﷺ) said:

نهى النبي —صلى الله عليه وسلم— عن بيع الغرر

"The Messenger of Allah (ﷺ) prohibited the Gharar sale."

As such, from all of the research I have conducted and the discussions I have had with 'Bitcoin believers', I feel strongly that it is impermissible to deal in Bitcoin and in this matter I favour the opinion and reasoning presented by Ustadh Abu Khaled Al Hejazi and Sheikh Ata bin Khalil Abu al-Rashtah. I am of the view the real investment opportunity in this field is not Bitcoin but rather innovative applications of Blockchain. Also, I am of the view that cryptocurrencies can indeed constitute currency and assets according to the *Shariah* assuming that they meet the conditions of these according to Islam correctly.

I conclude with the final example of when some Sahabah (ra) were apprehensive about the ban on polytheists coming near the Ka'bah, given that they worried of the destruction of their trade and the loss of their supplies. Therefore, Allah (swt) revealed,

"O you who believe! The polytheists are unclean, so let them not come near the Sacred Mosque after this year of theirs; and if you fear poverty, then Allah will enrich you from His Bounty if He wills."

We hope that all of us can understand and hold fast to these ayaat when it comes to the desire to engage in investments and transactions and act quickly due to thinking based on economic gains and loss as opposed to halal and haram.

Indeed Allah (swt) knows what benefits people and what harms them, and what amends them and what corrupts them,

$$\text{أَلَا يَعْلَمُ مَنْ خَلَقَ وَهُوَ اللَّطِيفُ الْخَبِيرُ}$$

"Should He not know, He that created? and He is the One that understands the finest mysteries (and) is well-acquainted (with them)."   [Al-Mulk: 14]

Your Brother
A.C. Ahmed
www.facebook.com/acahmed.page

www.ingramcontent.com/pod-product-compliance
Lightning Source LLC
Chambersburg PA
CBHW051336220526
45468CB00004B/1672